FIELDS'
REFERENCE
BOOK
of
NON-SEXIST
WORDS
and
PHRASES

Fields Enterprises, Inc.
Raleigh, North Carolina

Copyright © 1987 by Fields Enterprises, Inc.
3056 Granville Drive, Raleigh, North Carolina, 27609
Registered Copyright No. 185-942
Library of Congress Catalog Card Number 87-82768

First Edition
ISBN 0-944719-02-3

Table of Contents

Table of Contents

Foreword

In this Reference Book:

1. Distinctly different meanings of the same word are numbered.

2. Feminine word endings, such as ess, ette, enne and rix have been either eliminated or replaced by neutral word endings, such as or and an.

3. Use the word or phrase in the "Right" column <u>if you do not know whether a word or phrase refers to a male or female, or if it refers to both.</u>

A

Wrong	*Right*
Able Bodied Seaman	**Able Bodied Sailor; Able Bodied Mariner**
Able Seaman	**Able Sailor; Able Mariner**
Actress	**Actor**
Adman	**Advertiser; Ad Agent; Ad writer; Ad Solicitor; Ad Clerk; Ad Planner; Promoter**
Administra-trix	**Administrator**
Adulteress	**Adulterer**
Advance Man	**Advance Agent**

Wrong	*Right*
Adventuress	**Adventurer**
Advertising Man	**Advertiser; Advertising Agent; Advertising Writer; Advertising Solictor; Advertising Clerk; Advertising Planner; Promoter**
Airman	**Pilot; Aviator; Flier**
Airwoman	**Pilot; Aviator; Flier**
Adlerman	**Alderer; Alderperson; Town Board Member**
All Men Are Created Equal	**All Persons Are Created Equal; All People Are Created Equal; All Human Beings Are Created Equal**
Almsman	**Almsperson; Alms Recipient**

Wrong	Right
Altar Boy	**Altar Child; Altar Youth; Altar Youngster**
Alteration Lady	**Alterer**
Alumna	**Graduate; Attendee; Former Student**
Alumnae	**Graduates; Attendees; Former Students**
Alumni	**Graduates; Attendees; Former Students**
Alumnus	**Graduate; Attendee; Former Student**
Ambassadress	**Ambassador**
Ancestress	**Ancestor**
Anchoress	**Anchorite**
Anchorman	**Anchor; Anchorperson**
Anchorwoman	**Anchor; Anchorperson**

9

Wrong	Right
Artilleryman	**Artillerist**
As One Man	**As One Person**
Assemblyman	**Assembly Member**
Authoress	**Author**
Average Man	**Average Person**
Aviatrix	**Aviator; Pilot**

B

Wrong	*Right*
Batchelor	**Single**
Batchelor Girl	**Single**
Batchelorhood	**Singlehood**
Batchelor's Degree	**Baccalaureate Degree**
Baggageman	**Baggage Handler; Baggage Porter; Baggage Checker**
Bailsman	**Bailsperson**
Ballerina	**Ballet Dancer**
Bandmaster	**Band Leader; Band Conductor**

Eliminate "t" from Bachelor

Wrong	Right
Bandsman	**Band Player; Band Member**
Bargeman	**Barge Hand; Barge Captain**
Barmaid	**Bar Attendant; Bartender; Barserver; Bar Waiter; Bar Wait**
Barman	**Bar Attendant; Bartender; Barserver; Bar Waiter; Bar Wait**
Beachboy	**Beach Attendant**
Bellboy	**Bellhop; Bell Captain**
Bellman	**Bellhop; Bell Captain**
Benefactress	**Benefactor**
Be One's Own Man	**Be One's Own Person**
Boatman	**Boater**

Wrong	*Right*
Bogeyman	**Hobgoblin**
Bondman	**Slave**
Bondsman	**Bonder; Surety; Guarantor; Bondsperson**
Bondswoman	**Bonder; Surety; Guarantor; Bondsperson**
Bondwoman	**Slave**
Boogieman	**Hobgoblin**
Boogyman	**Hobgoblin**
Bookman	**Bookworm**
Bowman	**Archer**
Boy	**Baby; Child; Youth; Youngster; Teen-ager; Adolescent; Minor**
Boyfriend	**1. Friend; Close Friend; Sweetheart**

Wrong	Right
	2. Homemate; Housemate; Live-in; Long-time companion
Boyhood	Childhood
Boys' Choir	Children's Choir; Youth Choir
Brakeman	Braker; Brake Operator
Brother	Sibling
Brotherhood	1. Humanhood; Fellowship 2. Association; Organization; Union
Brotherhood of Man	Bond of Humanity; Bond of Humankind; Fellowship of Humanity; Human Kinship

Wrong	Right
Brotherly Love	**Human Love; Affectionate Love; Devoted Love**
Busboy	**Busperson**
Busgirl	**Busperson**
Businessman	**Businessperson; Executive; Manager**
Business-woman	**Businessperson; Executive; Manager**
Businessmen's Lunch	**Businesspersons' Lunch**
Businessmen's Meeting	**Businesspersons' Meeting**
Busman	**Bus Driver**

C

Wrong	*Right*
Cabinboy	**Cabin Attendant**
Callboy	**1. Caller; Page** **2. Prostitute**
Callgirl	**1. Caller; Page** **2. Prostitute**
Cameraman	**Camera Operator;** **Photographer;** **Videographer**
Cattleman	**Cattle Rancher;** **Cattle Owner;** **Cattle Raiser;** **Cattle Tender**
Caveman	**Cave Dweller**

Wrong	Right
Chairman	**Chair; Chairperson; Presiding Officer; Core Person; Coordinator; Convener; Moderator**
Chairmanship	**Chairship; Directorship; Headship**
Chairwoman	**Chair; Chairperson; Presiding Officer; Core person; Coordinator; Convener; Moderator**
Charlady	**Charworker; Cleaner**
Charwoman	**Charworker; Cleaner**
Checkout Boy	**Checker**
Checkout Girl	**Checker**
Checkroom Boy	**Checkroom Attendant; Checker**

Wrong	*Right*
Checkroom Girl	**Checkroom Attendant; Checker**
Choirboy	**Choir Child; Youth Choir Member; Children's Choir Member; Chorister**
Choirgirl	**Choir Child; Youth Choir Member; Children's Choir Member; Chorister**
Choirmaster	**Choir Director; Choir Leader**
Chorine	**Chorus Member**
Chorus Boy	**Chorus Member; Chorus Dancer/Singer; Chorister**

Wrong	Right
Chorus Girl	**Chorus Member; Chorus Dancer/Singer; Chorister**
Churchman	**Church Member; Churchgoer; Clergy Member**
Churchwoman	**Church Member; Churchgoer; Clergy Member**
Cigarette Girl	**Cigarette Vendor**
Citrus Man	**Citrus Grower**
City Father	**City Official; City Founder**
Clansman	**Clan Member**
Cleaning Lady	**Cleaner; Janitor; Domestic Worker**
Cleaning Man	**Cleaner; Janitor; Domestic Worker**

Wrong	*Right*
Cleaning Woman	**Cleaner; Janitor; Domestic Worker**
Clergyman	**Clergy Member; Cleric**
Clergywoman	**Clergy Member; Cleric**
Cloakroom Boy	**Cloakroom Attendant**
Cloakroom Girl	**Cloakroom Attendant**
Clubman	**Club Member; Clubber; Club Leader; Civic Leader; Joiner**
Clubwoman	**Club Member; Clubber; Club Leader; Civic Leader; Joiner**
Coachman	**Coach Driver**

Wrong	Right
Coastguards-man	**Coastguard Member; Coastguarder**
Coed	**Student**
Comedienne	**Comedian; Humorist**
Committeeman	**Committee Member**
Committee-woman	**Committee Member**
Common Man	**Commoner; Average Person; Ordinary Person; Common Person**
Concertmaster	**First Violinist; Assistant Conductor**
Conductress	**Conductor**
Confidence Man	**Con Artist; Swindler; Flimflammer**
Congressman	**Congress Member; Representative;**

Wrong	Right
	Senator; House Member; Senate Member
Congress-woman	Congress Member; Representative; Senator; House Member; Senate Member
Copyboy	Copy Carrier; Errand Runner; Gofer
Corpsman	Corps Member
Councilman	Council Member; Councilor
Councilwoman	Council Member; Councilor
Counterman	Counter Attendant
Counterwoman	Counter Attendant
Countryman	1. Fellow Citizen; Compatriot

Wrong	Right
	2. Country Dweller; Rural Dweller
Country-woman	1. Fellow Citizen; Compatriot 2. Country Dweller; Rural Dweller
Cowboy	Cowpoke; Cowhand; Cowpuncher; Cowherder
Cowboy Boots	Western Boots
Cowboy Hat	Western Hat
Cowboy Outfit	Western Outfit
Cowgirl	Cowpoke; Cowhand; Cowpuncher; Cowherder
Cowgirl Boots	Western Boots
Cowgirl Hat	Western Hat

Wrong	*Right*
Cowgirl Outfit	**Western Outfit**
Cowman	**Rancher**
Craftsman	**Crafter; Craftsperson; Craftsworker; Handcrafter**
Craftsmanlike	**Craftslike; Skillful**
Craftsmanship	**Craftship; Skill**
Craftswoman	**Crafter; Craftsperson; Craftsworker; Handcrafter**
Crewman	**Crew Member**

<u>D</u>

Wrong	Right
Dairymaid	**Dairy Worker; Dairy Employee**
Dairyman	**Dairy Operator; Dairy Farmer; Dairy owner; Dairy Manager**
Daughter	**Child**
Deaconess	**Deacon; Lay Officer**
Delivery Boy	**Delivery Person**
Delivery Girl	**Delivery Person**
Delivery Man	**Delivery Person**
Delivery Woman	**Delivery Person**

Wrong	*Right*
Deskman	**Desk Person**
Deskwoman	**Desk Person**
Detail Man	**Detail Representative**
Directress	**Director**
Dirty Old Man	Lecher
Divorcé	**Single**
Divorcée	**Single**
Doorman	**Doorkeeper**
Doughboy	Soldier
Draftsman	**Drafter**
Draftswoman	**Drafter**
Draughtsman	**Drafter**
Drayman	**Drayer; Hauler**
Drillmaster	**Drill Instructor**

Wrong	*Right*
Drum Majorette	**Drum Major**
Dustman	**Trash Collector**

<u>E</u>

Wrong	*Right*
Editress	**Editor**
Elder Statesman	**Elder Statesperson**
Enchantress	**1. Enchanter; Sorcerer** **2. Enchanting Person**
End Man	**End Person**
Englishmen	**The English**
Enlisted Man	**Enlistee**
Equestrienne	**Equestrian**
Errand Boy	**Errand Runner**
Errand Girl	**Errand Runner**

Wrong	Right
Everyman	1. **Moralist**
	2. **Average Person; Typical Human Being; Ordinary Person**
Exciseman	**Excise Tax Collector**
Executrix	**Executor**
Expressman	**Expresser**

F

Wrong	Right
Faggot	Homosexual
Fall Guy	Scapegoat; Dupe
Family of Man	Human Family; Global Neighbors
Farmerette	Farmer
Father	Parent
Fatherhood	Parenthood
Fatherhood of God	Godhood
Fatherland	Homeland
Father Time	Time

Wrong	*Right*
Fellow Countryman	**Fellow Citizen; Compatriot**
Fellowman	**Fellow Human Being; Fellow Citizen; Compatriot**
Ferryman	**Ferry Operator; Ferry Hand; Ferry Owner**
Fiancé	**Betrothed**
Fiancée	**Betrothed**
Fireman	**Firefighter**
Fisherman	**Fisher; Angler**
Flagman	**Flagger; Signaler**
Flagwoman	**Flagger; Signaler**
Fly-boy	**Flier (Flyer); Pilot; Aviator**
Foeman	**Foe; Enemy**

Wrong	Right
Foilsman	Fencer
Footboy	Page; Servant
Footman	Liveried Servant
Forefather	Forebear; Founder; Ancestor; Forerunner
Forelady	1. Supervisor; Manager; Overseer 2. Head Juror
Foreman	1. Supervisor; Manager; Overseer 2. Head Juror
Foremother	Forebear; Founder; Ancestor; Forerunner
Forewoman	1. Supervisor; Manager; Overseer 2. Head Juror
Founding Father	Founder; Pioneer; Colonist

Wrong	_Right_
Founding Mother	**Founder; Pioneer; Colonist**
Freedwoman	**Freedperson**
Freedman	**Freedperson**
Freeman	**Freeperson; Citizen**
Freewoman	**Freeperson; Citizen**
Frenchmen	**The French**
Freshman	**1. Frosh; First Year Student; Newcomer** **2. Novice**
Frogman	**Underwater Swimmer; Frog Swimmer**
Frontiersman	**Frontier Settler; Frontier Dweller; Pioneer**

Wrong	*Right*
Frontiers-woman	**Frontier Settler; Frontier Dweller; Pioneer**
Front Man	**Front**
Fugleman	**Model; Leader**
Funnyman	**Comedian; Humorist; Clown**
Funnywoman	**Comedian; Humorist; Clown**

G

Wrong	Right
Gagman	**Gag Writer; Gagster**
Gamesman-ship	**Gameship; Gamescraft**
Garbageman	**Garbage Collector**
Gateman	**Gate Tender; Gatekeeper**
Gentleman	**Gentleperson; Courteous Person; Aristocrat**
Gentleman Farmer	**Gentle Farmer; Absentee Farmer**
Gentlemanlike	**Well-bred; Distinguished;**

Wrong	Right
	Aristocratic; Courteous; Proper; Elegant
Gentleman of Fortune	**Adventurer**
Gentleman's Agreement	**Handshake Agreement; Honorable Agreement; Informal Agreement; Promise; Word of Honor**
Gentleman's Gentleman	**Valet; Servant**
Gentlewoman	**Gentleperson; Courteous Person; Aristocrat**
Girl	**Baby; Child; Youth; Youngster; Teen-ager; Adolescent; Minor**
Girl Friday	**Right-arm; Aide**

Wrong	Right
Girlfriend	1. Friend; Close Friend; Sweetheart 2. Homemate; Housemate; Live-in; Long-time Companion
Girlhood	Childhood; Youth
Girls' Choir	Children's Choir; Youth Choir
G-man	Government Agent
Goddaughter	Godchild
Godson	Godchild
God the Father	God; Godhead; Creator; Spirit of God; Deity
Goodman	Head of Household
Governess	Resident Tutor
Grade Mother	Grade Parent

Wrong	Right
Grass Widow	**Single**
Grass Widower	**Single**
Groomsman	**Usher**
Guardsman	**Guard**
Guildsman	**Guilder**
Gunman	**Gunner; Shooter**

H

Wrong	Right
Hackman	**Driver**
Handicrafts-man	**Handcrafter; Handcraft Worker; Artisan**
Handmaid	**Servant**
Handyman	**Handyperson; Odd-jobber; Fixer**
Hangman	**Executioner**
Harbormaster	**Harbor Manager; Harbor Supervisor; Harbor Director**

Wrong	Right
Hat Check Girl	**Hat Checker; Hat Check Attendant**
Hatchetman	**Thug; Hired Gun; Mobster; Gangster**
Headman	**Boss; Head Person; Manager**
Head Master	**Head; Principal; Director**
Head Mistress	**Head; Principal; Director**
Headsman	**Executioner**
Heiress	**Heir**
Helmsman	**Steerer**
Henchman	**1. Mobster; Thug; Gangster** **2. Subordinate; Supporter**
Herdsman	**Herder**

Wrong	*Right*
Heritress	**Heir; Inheritor**
Heroine	**Hero**
High Priestess	**High Priest**
Highwayman	**Highway Robber**
History of Man	**History of Humankind; History of the Human Race**
Hit Man	**Hit; Thug; Hired Gun; Mobster; Gangster**
Homeroom Mother	**Homeroom Parent**
Horseman	**Equestrian; Horse Rider; Horse Breeder; Horse Trainer; Jockey**
Horsemanship	**Horseship; Equitation**
Horsewoman	**Equestrian; Horse Rider; Horse Breeder;**

Wrong	Right
	Horse Trainer; Jockey
Hostess	**Host**
Houseboy	**Servant**
Housefather	**Houseparent**
Househusband	**Homemaker; House Spouse; Householder**
Housemaid	**Servant**
Housemaster	**House Manager**
Housemother	**Houseparent**
Housewife	**Homemaker; House Spouse; Householder**
Huntress	**Hunter**
Huntsman	**Hunter**

Wrong	*Right*
Husband	**Spouse**
Husbandman	**Farmer**

I

Wrong	Right
Iceman	**Ice Carrier; Ice Vendor**
Infantryman	**Infantry Soldier; Foot Soldier**
Inner Man	**Inner Self**
Instructress	**Instructor**
Insurance Man	**Insurance Agent**
Irishmen	**The Irish**

<u>L</u>

Wrong	*Right*
Ladies' Auxiliary	**Auxiliary**
Ladies' Man	**Flirt; Charmer; Tempter; Smooth Talker; Courter; Seducer; Lover**
Ladies' Room	**Restroom; Necessary Room**
Lady	**Gentleperson; Courteous Person; Aristocrat**
Lady Accountant	**Accountant**

Wrong	Right
Lady Architect	**Architect**
Lady Attorney	**Attorney**
Lady Dentist	**Dentist**
Lady Doctor	**Doctor**
Lady Engineer	**Engineer**
Lady Insurance Agent	**Insurance Agent**
Lady in Waiting	**Attendant in Waiting**
Lady Killer	**Flirt; Charmer; Tempter; Smooth Talker; Courter; Seducer; Lover**
Ladylike	**Well-bred; Distinguished; Aristocratic; Courteous; Proper; Elegant**

Wrong	*Right*
Lady Love	**Loved One**
Lady of the House	**Head of the House**
Lady Pharmacist	**Pharmacist**
Lady Physician	**Physician**
Lady Professor	**Professor**
Lady Realtor	**Realtor**
Lady Steelworker	**Steelworker**
Landlady	1. **Landowner; Property Owner;** 2. **Manager**
Landlord	1. **Landowner; Property Owner;** 2. **Manager**
Landsman	**Farmer**

Wrong	Right
Laundress	**Launderer; Laundry Worker**
Laundryman	**Launderer; Laundry Worker**
Lawman	**Law Officer**
Layman	**Lay Person**
Laywoman	**Lay Person**
Leading Lady	**Leading Actor**
Leading Man	**Leading Actor**
Legman	**Scout; Gofer; Informer; Subordinate**
Lesbian	**Homosexual**
Lineman/ Linesman	**1. Lineworker; Line Repairer; Line Installer** **2. Line Player; Line Official**

Wrong	Right
Linkboy	**Linker; Torch Bearer**
Linkman	**Linker; Torch Bearer**
Linksman	**Golfer**
Lioness	**Lion**
Liveryman	**Livery Keeper**
Lobsterman	**Lobsterer**
Longshoreman	**Stevedore; Longshore Worker; Dock Worker; Dockhand**
Lord	**1. Creator; God; Sovereign 2. Noble Person**
Lumberman	**Lumberer; Lumber Dealer**

<u>M</u>

Wrong	*Right*
Madam Chairman	**Chair; Chairperson**
Madman	**Lunatic**
Madwoman	**Lunatic**
Maid	**Domestic; Servant; Room Cleaner**
Maiden	**1. Single; Unmarried** **2. First; Initial; Earliest**
Maidenhood	**Singlehood**
Maidenly	**Youthful**

Wrong	Right
Maiden Name	**Birth Surname; Family Name; Former Name**
Maiden Voyage	**First Voyage; Initial Voyage; Earliest Voyage**
Maid in Waiting	**Attendant in Waiting; Courtier**
Maidservant	**Household Servant; Domestic**
Maid Service	**Domestic Service**
Mailman	**Mail Carrier; Letter Carrier; Postal Carrier; Postal Clerk**
Maintenance Man	**Maintenance Person; Maintenance Engineer; Repairer; Fixer; Mender; Handyperson**

Wrong	Right
Majorette	1. **Drum Major** 2. **Baton Twirler**
Man	1. **Human** 2. **Staff; Operate;** **Serve at/on**
Manageress	**Manager**
Man-day	**Day; Work-day**
Man-eater	**Human-eater; Cannibal;** **Carnivore**
Man Friday	**Right-arm; Aide**
Manful	**Humanful**
Manhandle	**Mistreat; Abuse**
Manhole	**Utility Hole; Access Hole**
Manhood	**Humanhood; Adulthood;** **Personhood**
Man-hour	**Hour; Work-hour**
Manhunt	**Hunt; Search**

Wrong	Right
Man in the Street	**Person in the Street; Average Person; Typical Person; Layperson**
Mankind	**Humankind; Humanity; Human Family; Human Beings; Mortals; People; Human Race; Human Society**
Mankind's Achievements	**Humankind's Achievements; Humanity's Achievements; Mortal's Achievements; People's Achievements**
Manlike	**Humanlike**
Manliness	**Humanness**
Manly	**Humanly; Courageous; Valiant**

Wrong	Right
Manmade	**Humanmade; Synthetic; Artificial; Manufactured; Machine-made; Hand-made; Fabricated; Constructed**
Manned	**Staffed**
Manned Space Flight	**Staffed Space Flight**
Mannish	**Humanish; Androgynous**
Man of God	**Cleric; Preacher; Minister; Rabbi; Priest; Guru**
Man of Letters	**Scholar**
Man of the Cloth	**Cleric**
Man of the House	**Head of the House; Householder**

Wrong	*Right*
Man of the World	**Worldly Person; Sophisticate**
Man-on-Man	**One-on-One**
Manpower	**Humanpower; Peoplepower; Musclepower; Brainpower; Workers; Staff; Personnel; Work Force; Human Resources**
Man-rate	**Rate; Work-rate**
Manservant	**Servant**
Man's Inhumanity to Man	**Human's Inhumanity to Human**
Man-sized	**Human-sized**
Manslaughter	**Humanslaughter**

Wrong	Right
Manslayer	**Humanslayer**
Man Space	**Human Space**
Man's Rights	**Human Rights**
Man-to-man	**Person-to-person**
Mantrap	**Trap; Humantrap**
Manward	**Humanward**
Manwise	**Humanwise**
Marksman	**Sharpshooter**
Marksmanship	**Marksship; Markscraft**
Markswoman	**Sharpshooter**
Masseur	**Massager; Physiotherapist**
Masseuse	**Massager; Physiotherapist**
Master	**1. Ruler; Leader; Head; Owner; Teacher;**

Wrong	Right
	Principal; Superior
	2. Authority; Champion; Winner; Expert; Greatest
	3. Model; Original; Prototype
	4. Conquer; Overcome; Dominate; Control
Master Bath	Principal Bath; Main Bath
Master Bedroom	Principal Bedroom; Main Bedroom
Master Craftsman	Skilled Crafter; Head Crafter
Masterful	1. Skillful; Excellent
	2. Domineering; Authoritative
Masterhand	Skilled Hand; Old Hand; Expert

Wrong	*Right*
Master Key	**Common Key**
Masterly	1. **Skillful; Excellent**
	2. **Authoritative; Domineering**
Mastermind	1. **Creator; Originator; Innovator; Intellectual; Genius**
	2. **Direct; Plan; Supervise**
Master of Arts	**Intermediate Graduate Degree of Arts**
Master of Ceremonies	**Host; Presider; Marshal**
Master of Science	**Intermediate Graduate Degree of Science**
Masterpiece	**Great Piece/Work/ Creation; Classic**
Master Plan	**Model Plan; Prototype**

Wrong	Right
Mastership	**Expertise; Proficiency**
Masterstroke	**Stroke of Genius**
Mastery	1. **Control; Command** 2. **Expertise; Knowledge; Skill**
Mayoress	**Mayor**
Meatman	**Butcher; Meat Cutter**
Mediatress	**Mediator**
Mediatrice	**Mediator**
Mediatrix	**Mediator**
Medicine Man	**Witch Doctor; Medicine Healer**
Men at Work	**People Working**
Men Working	**People Working**
Men's Room	**Restroom; Necessary Room**

Wrong	_Right_
Merchantman	**Merchant Ship**
Mermaid	**Sea Nymph**
Merman	**Sea Nymph**
Meter Maid	**Meter Reader;** **Meter Officer;** **Meter Checker;** **Meter Attendant**
Meter Man	**Meter Reader;** **Meter Officer;** **Meter Checker;** **Meter Attendant**
Middleman	**Middleperson;** **Middle Processor;** **Intermediary;** **Go-between; Liaison;** **Interceder; Wholesaler;** **Jobber; Broker**
Midshipman	**Naval Cadet;** **Midshipperson**

Wrong	*Right*
Midwife	**Birthing Assistant**
Milady	**Gentleperson**
Militiaman	**Militia Member**
Milkmaid	**Milker**
Milkman	**Milk Carrier**
Millionairess	**Millionaire**
Missileman	**Missile Designer;** **Missile Builder;** **Missile Operator;** **Missile Launcher**
Mistress	1. **Ruler; Leader; Head;** **Owner; Teacher;** **Principal; Superior;** 2. **Authority; Champion;** **Expert** 3. **Fornicator;** **Long-time Companion**
Mistress of Ceremonies	**Host; Presider; Marshal**

Wrong	Right
Modern Man	**Modern Human;** **Modern Humanity;** **Modern Civilization;** **Modern People**
Mother	**Parent**
Mother Church	**Church**
Mother Earth	**Earth**
Motherland	**Homeland**
Mother Nature	**Nature**
Motorman	**Train/Tram/Subway Operator**

<u>N</u>

Wrong	*Right*
Narratrix	**Narrator**
Needlewoman	**Sewer; Seamster; Tailor; Artisan; Crafter**
Negress	**Negro; Black**
Newsboy	**News Carrier; Newspaper Carrier; Newspaper Vendor; Newspaper Deliverer; Newspaper Seller**
Newsman	**Newscaster; News Reporter; News Writer; News Editor**

Wrong	Right
Newspaper-man	Newspaper Reporter; Newspaper Writer; Newspaper Editor; Newspaper Employee
Newspaper-woman	Newspaper Reporter; Newspaper Writer; Newspaper Editor; Newspaper Employee
Newswoman	Newscaster; News Reporter; News Writer; News Editor
Night Watchman	Night Watcher; Night Guard; Security Guard; Night Keeper; Night Sentry
Nobleman	Nobleperson
Noblewoman	Nobleperson

Wrong	*Right*
No Man's Land	**No One's Land; Buffer Zone**
Nursemaid	**Child's Nurse**

O

Wrong	*Right*
Oarsman	**Rower; Racing Crew Member**
Oarsmanship	**Oarsship; Oarscraft**
Office Boy	**Office Helper; Office Employee; Office Worker**
Office Girl	**Office Helper; Office Employee; Office Worker**
Oilman	**Oil Tycoon; Oil Driller; Oil Dealer; Oil Seller**
Old Lady	**1. Old Person** **2. Spouse**

Wrong	Right
Old Maid	**Single**
Old Man	**1. Old Person** **2. Spouse**
Old Wives' Tale	**Tale; Myth; Superstition; Folklore**
Ombudsman	**Ombudsperson**
Ombuds-woman	**Ombudsperson**
One-man	**One-person**
One Man-One Vote	**One Person-One Vote**
One Man Show	**One Person Show**
One's Own Man	**One's Own Person**
One-upman-ship	**One-upship**

Wrong	Right
Orchardman	**Orchardist**
Ordinary Seaman	**Ordinary Sailor; Deckhand**
Organization Man	**Organization Person**
Outdoorsman	**Outdoorsperson**
Outdoorsman-ship	**Outdoorsship; Outdoorscraft**
Overman	**Supervisor**
Oysterman	**Oysterer; Oyster Opener; Oyster Worker; Oyster Cultivator; Oyster Vendor**

P

Wrong	Right
Packman	**Peddler; Vendor**
Pageboy	**Page**
Pagegirl	**Page**
Pantryman	**Pantry Manager; Pantry Worker**
Paperboy	**Paper Carrier; Paper Vendor**
Past Master	**Expert**
Past Mistress	**Expert**
Patrolman	**Trooper; Patrol Officer; Police Officer; Patroller**
Patroness	**Patron**

Wrong	Right
Paymaster	**Payer; Pay Officer; Pay Agent**
Peace On Earth, Goodwill To Men	**Peace On Earth, Goodwill To All**
Penman	**Scribe; Copyist; Calligrapher; Writer**
Penmanship	**Penship; Pencraft; Handwriting**
Pilgram Fathers	**Pilgrims**
Pitchman	**Peddler; Street Vendor; Concessionaire**
Pitman	**Pit Worker; Coal Miner**
Pivotman	**Pivot**
Plainclothes-man	**Plainclothesperson; Detective; Investigator; Undercover Agent**

Wrong	*Right*
Plainsman	**Plainsdweller**
Playboy	**Hedonist; Pleasure Seeker**
Playgirl	**Hedonist; Pleasure Seeker**
Plebette	**Plebe**
Plowman	**Plower**
Poetess	**Poet**
Point Man	**Point Person**
Policeman	**Police Officer; Member of the Police Force**
Policewoman	**Police Officer; Member of the Police Force**
Poor Boy	**Poor Person**

Wrong	*Right*
Postman	**Mail Carrier;** **Letter Carrier;** **Postal Carrier;** **Postal Clerk**
Postmaster	**Postal Chief;** **Head of the Post Office**
Postmistress	**Postal Chief;** **Head of the Post Office**
Potboy	**Potperson**
Prehistoric Man	**Prehistoric Human;** **Prehistoric Person**
Pressman	1. **Member of the Press** 2. **Press Agent** 3. **Press Operator**
Presswoman	1. **Member of the Press** 2. **Press Agent** 3. **Press Operator**
Priestess	**Priest**

Wrong	*Right*
Primitive Man	**Primitive Human;** **Primitive Person**
Procuress	**Procurer**
Program Chairman	**Program Chair;** **Program Chairperson**
Property Man	**Property Hand;** **Property Person**
Prophetess	**Prophet**
Prop Man	**Prop Hand; Prop Person**
Proprietress	**Proprietor**
Protectress	**Protector**

Q

Wrong	Right
Quarryman	**Quarrier; Quarry Worker**
Queen	**Ruler; Monarch; Sovereign**

R

Wrong	Right
Radioman	**Radio Operator;** **Radio Technician;** **Radio Engineer**
Raftsman	**Rafter; Raft Worker**
Ragman	**Rag Collector;** **Rag Dealer**
Ranchman	**Rancher; Ranch Worker**
Renaissance Man	**Renaissance Person**
Repairman	**Repairer**
Rewrite Man	**Rewriter**

Wrong	*Right*
Rifleman	**Rifle Shooter; Sharpshooter**
Right-hand Man	**Right Hand**
Rights of Man	**Human Rights**
Roadman	**Road Worker**
Rodman	**Rod Holder; Surveyor's Assistant**
Roundsman	**1. Patroller** **2. Circuit Rider**
Routeman	**Route Worker; Route Carrier**

S

Wrong	Right
Safetyman	**Safety**
Sailing Master	**Sailing Expert**
Salesgirl	**Salesperson; Salesclerk; Sales Representative; Sales Agent**
Saleslady	**Salesperson; Salesclerk; Sales Representative; Sales Agent**
Salesman	**Salesperson; Salesclerk; Sales Representative; Sales Agent**
Salesmanship	**Salesship; Salescraft**

Wrong	*Right*
Salesmen	**Salesforce; Salesstaff; Salespeople**
Saleswoman	**Salesperson; Salesclerk; Sales Representative; Sales Agent**
Saleswomen	**Salesforce; Salesstaff; Salespeople**
Sandman	**Sand Fairy; Sleep Fairy**
Sandwich Man	**Sandwich-board Carrier; Picketer**
Schoolboy	**School Child**
Schoolgirl	**School Child**
Schoolman	**Teacher; Educator**
Schoolmarm	**Teacher; Educator**
Schoolmaster	**School Teacher; Educator; Principal**

Wrong	*Right*
Schoolmistress	**School Teacher; Educator; Principal**
Scoutmaster	**Scout Leader**
Scrubwoman	**Scrubber; Cleaner**
Sculptress	**Sculptor**
Seaman	**Sailor; Mariner**
Seamstress	**Sewer; Seamster**
Second-story Man	**Burglar**
Secret Service Man	**Secret Service Agent**
Seductress	**Seducer**
Seedsman	**Sower; Seed Dealer**
Seeress	**Seer; Prophet; Clairvoyant; Soothsayer**

Wrong	Right
Selectman	**Selectperson; Town Councilor; Town Official**
Separate the Men from the Boys	**Separate the Adults from the Children**
Serviceman	**1. Military Person** **2. Repairer; Servicer** **3. Service Station Attendant**
Shantyman	**Shantyperson**
Shepherdess	**Shepherd**
Shipman	**Sailor**
Shipmaster	**Ship Captain; Ship Commander**
Shoeshine Boy	**Shoeshiner**
Shovelman	**Shoveler**

Wrong	Right
Showman	Showperson; Entertainer
Showmanship	Showship
Sideman	Jazz Musician
Signalman	Signaler
Sister	Sibling
Sisterhood	1. Personhood; Humanhood; Fellowship 2. Association; Organization; Union
Sisterly Love	Love; Human Love; Affectionate Love; Devoted Love
Snow Man	Snow Sculpture
Sob Sister	1. Sob-story Writer 2. Sentimentalist

Wrong	Right
Son	**Child**
Sonarman	**Sonar Operator**
Songstress	**Singer; Vocalist; Songster**
Son of Man	**Human One; Human Being; Messiah**
Sorceress	**Sorcerer**
Spaceman	**Space Traveler**
Spacewoman	**Space Traveler**
Spectatress	**Spectator**
Spinster	**Single**
Spoilsman	**Spoils Recipient; Spoils Splitter**
Spokesman	**Spokesperson; Representative**

Wrong	*Right*
Spokeswoman	**Spokesperson; Representative**
Sportsman	**Sportsperson**
Sportsmanship	**Sportsship**
Sportswoman	**Sportsperson**
Stableboy	**Stablehand**
Stablelad	**Stablehand**
Stableman	**Stablehand**
Starlet	**Aspirant Star; Actor**
Statesman	**Statesperson**
Statesmanlike	**Stateslike**
Statesmanship	**Statesship**
Stateswoman	**Statesperson**
Stationmaster	**Station Manager; Station Official**

Wrong	_Right_
Steersman	**Steerer; Pilot**
Steward	**Flight Attendant**
Stewardess	**Flight Attendant**
Stickman	1. **Stick Figure** 2. **Stick Handler** **Stick Player**
Stillman	**Still Operator**
Stockman	1. **Stocker;** **Stockperson;** **Stockworker** 2. **Stocktender;** **Stockowner**
Storeman	**Storekeeper**
Straightman	**Straightliner**
Strawman	1. **Strawperson** 2. **Scarecrow**
Stuntman	**Stuntperson;** **Stunt Performer**

Wrong	Right
Suffragette	**Suffragist**
Superman	**Superhuman**
Swagman	**Hobo; Vagrant**
Switchman	**Switcher; Switch Operator**
Swordsman	**Fencer; Swordsperson**
Swordsman-ship	**Swordsship; Swordscraft**

T

Wrong	Right
Tailoress	**Tailor**
Talesman	**Juror**
Tallyman	**Tallier; Scorekeeper; Recorder**
Taskmaster	**Boss; Task Assignor; Supervisor; Overseer**
Taskmistress	**Boss; Task Assignor; Supervisor; Overseer**
Temptress	**Tempter**
Testatrix	**Testator**
Tigress	**Tiger**

Wrong	*Right*
Tillerman	1. Steerer 2. Cultivator
Timberman	Timberworker; Lumberworker; Lumberjack
Tinman	Tinsmith
Tirewoman	Attirer
T-man	Treasury Agent
Toastmaster	Toastperson; Toastchair; Presider
Toastmistress	Toastperson; Toastchair; Presider
Tobaccoman	Tobacconist
Tollman	Toll Collector
Torchman	Torch

Wrong	*Right*
Townsman	**Townsperson**
Townswoman	**Townsperson**
Trackman	**1. Trackrunner** **2. Track Repairer**
Tradesman	**1. Trader; Shopkeeper** **2. Artisan; Crafter**
Tragedienne	**Tragedian**
Trainman	**Railroader;** **Trainworker;** **Train Crew Member**
Trainmaster	**Train Supervisor**
Traitoress	**Traitor**
Traitress	**Traitor**
Trashman	**Trash Collector;** **Trash Hauler;** **Trash Carrier**

Wrong	Right
Traveling Salesman	**Traveling Salesperson; Traveling Sales Representative**
Trawlerman	**Trawler**
Trencherman	**Hearty Eater**
Tribesman	**Tribe Member**
Triggerman	**Hired Gun; Gangster**
Truckman	**Trucker; Truck Driver**
Tutoress	**Tutor**

U

Wrong	Right
Underclass-man	**Under-class Member; Frosh; Sophomore**
Undercover Man	**Undercover Agent**
Undermanned	**Understaffed**
Unmanly	**Cowardly**
Unmanned	**Untended; Unstaffed**
Upperclass-man	**Upper-class Member; Junior; Senior**
Usherette	**Usher**
Unsportsman-like	**Unsportslike**

Wrong	_Right_
Unworkman-like	**Unworkerlike**
Upmanship	**One-upship**
Utility Man	**Utilitarianist; Utility Person**

V

Wrong	Right
Venire-man	**Venire Member**
Vestryman	**Vestry Member**
Victress	**Victor**
Villainess	**Villain**
Visiting Fireman	**Visiting VIP; Important Visitor**
Votaress	**Votary**

W

Wrong	*Right*
Waitress	**Waiter; Wait; Wait Person; Server**
Wardress	**Warden**
Wardrobe Mistress	**Wardrobe Supervisor**
Warehouse-man	**Warehouser**
Washerman	**Washer; Launderer**
Washwoman	**Washer; Launderer**
Watchman	**Watchguard; Watch; Guard; Lookout; Security Guard**

Wrong	*Right*
Waterboy	**Water Carrier**
Waterman	**Watercrafter; Boater**
Watermanship	**Watership; Watercraft**
Weathergirl	**Weathercaster; Weather Reporter**
Weatherman	**Weathercaster; Weather Reporter**
Weather-woman	**Weathercaster; Weather Reporter**
Weightman	**Weight Lifter; Weight Thrower**
Wharfmaster	**Wharf Manager**
Wheelman	**Steerer; Navigator; Driver; Cyclist**
Wheelsman	**Steerer; Navigator; Driver; Cyclist**
White Man's Burden	**White People's Burden**

Wrong	Right
Widow	**Surviving Spouse**
Widower	**Surviving Spouse**
Widowerhood	**Survivorhood**
Widowhood	**Survivorhood**
Wife	**Spouse**
Wireman	**Wire Repairer;** **Wire Stringer;** **Line Repairer;** **Line Stringer**
Witch	**Sorcerer; Conjuror**
Woodsman	**1. Woodcrafter** **2. Forester** **3. Woods Lover**
Woman	**Human**
Womanhood	**Humanhood;** **Adulthood;** **Personhood**

Wrong	Right
Woman-hour	**Hour; Work-hour**
Womanish	**Humanish; Androgynous**
Womanize	**Humanize**
Womankind	**Humankind; Humanity; Human Family; Human Beings; Mortals; People; Human Race; Human Society**
Womankind's Achievements	**Humankind's Achievements; Humanity's Achievements; Mortal's Achievements; People's Achievements**
Womanlike	**Humanlike**
Womanliness	**Humanness**
Womanly	**Humanly; Courageous; Valiant**

Wrong	Right
Woman of the Street	**Prostitute**
Womanpower	**Humanpower; Peoplepower; Musclepower; Brainpower; Workers; Staff; Personnel; Work Force; Human Resources**
Woman Servant	**Servant**
Woman-sized	**Human-sized**
Woman's Rights	**Human's Rights**
Women's Auxiliary	**Auxiliary**
Women's Room	**Restroom; Necessary Room**

Wrong	Right
Workingman	**Worker**
Workman	**Worker**
Workmanlike	**Workerlike**
Workmanship	**Workership**
Workmen's Compensation Insurance	**Workers' Compensation Insurance**
Workwoman	**Worker**

<u>Y</u>

Wrong	*Right*
Yachtsman	**Yachter**
Yardman	**1. Yardperson; Yardworker; Yardhand** **2. Yard Supervisor**
Yardmaster	**Yard Supervisor**
Yeoman	**Farmer**
Yeomanry	**Freeholders**
Yeoman Service	**Loyal Service; Great Service**
Yes Man	**Yes Person**

APPENDIX I
Reference to Persons and Animals

When using a word referring to a person or animal and you do not know whether the word refers to a male or female, do not refer to the word unless absolutely necessary. If reference is necessary, repeat the word or use the right reference word, as in:

Wrong	*Right*

ACROBAT
He, IIim, His   **He or She, Him or Her, His or Her**

ADOLESCENT
He, Him, His   **He or She, Him or Her, His or Her**

ADULT
He, Him, His   **He or She, Him or Her, His or Her**

Wrong	Right

ANIMAL
He, Him, His   It,   It,   Its

APPLICANT
He, Him, His   He or She, Him or Her,
His or Her

ARTIST
He, Him, His   He or She, Him or Her,
His or Her

ATTORNEY
He, Him, His   He or She, Him or Her,
His or Her

AUCTIONEER
He, Him, His   He or She, Him or Her,
His or Her

AUDITOR
He, Him, His   He or She, Him or Her,
His or Her

AUTHOR
He, Him, His   He or She, Him or Her,
His or Her

Wrong	*Right*

BABY
He, Him, His   **He or She, Him or Her, His or Her**

BABY SITTER
She, Her, Her   **He or She, Him or Her, His or Her**

BOOKKEEPER
She, Her, Her   **He or She, Him or Her, His or Her**

BRICKLAYER
He, Him, His   **He or She, Him or Her, His or Her**

CARPENTER
He, Him, His   **He or She, Him or Her, His or Her**

CHAUFFEUR
He, Him, His   **He or She, Him or Her, His or Her**

Wrong	Right

CHEF
He, Him, His　　He or She, Him or Her, His or Her

CHILD
He, Him, His　　He or She, Him or Her, His or Her

CITIZEN
He, Him, His　　He or She, Him or Her, His or Her

COACH
He, Him, His　　He or She, Him or Her, His or Her

COLONIST
He, Him, His　　He or She, Him or Her, His or Her

CONDUCTOR
He, Him, His　　He or She, Him or Her, His or Her

Wrong	*Right*

CONSUMER
He, Him, His   **He or She, Him or Her, His or Her**

CONTRACTOR
He, Him, His   **He or She, Him or Her, His or Her**

COOK
She, Her, Her   **He or She, Him or Her, His or Her**

DENTIST
He, Him, His   **He or She, Him or Her, His or Her**

DIETICIAN
She, Her, Her   **He or She, Him or Her, His or Her**

DIRECTOR
He, Him, His   **He or She, Him or Her, His or Her**

Wrong	Right

DOCK WORKER
He, Him, His **He or She, Him or Her, His or Her**

DOCTOR
He, Him, His **He or She, Him or Her, His or Her**

EDITOR
He, Him, His **He or She, Him or Her, His or Her**

ELECTRICIAN
He, Him, His **He or She, Him or Her, His or Her**

ENGINEER
He, Him, His **He or She, Him or Her, His or Her**

EXPLORER
He, Him, His **He or She, Him or Her, His or Her**

FARM OPERATOR
He, Him, His　　He or She, Him or Her, His or Her

FARMER
He, Him, His　　He or She, Him or Her, His or Her

FETUS
He, Him, His　　He or She, Him or Her, His or Her

FLYER
He, Him, His　　He or She, Him or Her, His or Her

FORTUNE TELLER
She, Her, Her　　He or She, Him or Her, His or Her

GARMENTWORKER
She, Her, Her　　He or She, Him or Her, His or Her

Wrong	*Right*

HELPER
He, Him, His   **He or She, Him or Her, His or Her**

HIRED HAND
He, Him, His   **He or She, Him or Her, His or Her**

IMMIGRANT
He, Him, His   **He or She, Him or Her, His or Her**

INDIVIDUAL
He, Him, His   **He or She, Him or Her, His or Her**

INFANT
He, Him, His   **He or She, Him or Her, His or Her**

INSURANCE AGENT
He, Him, His   **He or She, Him or Her, His or Her**

Wrong	Right

LABORER
He, Him, His **He or She, Him or Her, His or Her**

NOMAD
He, Him, His **He or She, Him or Her, His or Her**

NURSE
She, Her, Her **He or She, Him or Her, His or Her**

OCCUPANT
He, Him, His **He or She, Him or Her, His or Her**

OFFICIAL
He, Him, His **He or She, Him or Her, His or Her**

PAINTER
He, Him, His **He or She, Him or Her, His or Her**

Wrong	*Right*

PATIENT
He, Him, His   **He or She, Him or Her, His or Her**

PHOTOGRAPHER
He, Him, His   **He or She, Him or Her, His or Her**

PIECEWORKER
She, Her, Her   **He or She, Him or Her, His or Her**

PILOT
He, Him, His   **He or She, Him or Her, His or Her**

PIONEER
He, Him, His   **He or She, Him or Her, His or Her**

PLUMBER
He, Him, His   **He or She, Him or Her, His or Her**

Wrong	*Right*

POLITICIAN
He, Him, His   **He or She, Him or Her, His or Her**

PROFESSOR
He, Him, His   **He or She, Him or Her, His or Her**

RESIDENT
He, Him, His   **He or She, Him or Her, His or Her**

SCIENTIST
He, Him, His   **He or She, Him or Her, His or Her**

SECRETARY
She, Her, Her   **He or She, Him or Her, His or Her**

SETTLER
He, Him, His   **He or She, Him or Her, His or Her**

Wrong	*Right*

SHOPPER
She, Her, Her · **He or She, Him or Her, His or Her**

SLAVE
He, Him, His · **He or She, Him or Her, His or Her**

STEELWORKER
He, Him, His · **He or She, Him or Her, His or Her**

SURGEON
He, Him, His · **He or She, Him or Her, His or Her**

TEACHER
She, Her, Her · **He or She, Him or Her, His or Her**

TEAMSTER
He, Him, His · **He or She, Him or Her, His or Her**

Wrong	*Right*

TEEN-AGER
He, Him, His   **He or She, Him or Her, His or Her**

TRAVELER
He, Him, His   **He or She, Him or Her, His or Her**

VOTER
He, Him, His   **He or She, Him or Her, His or Her**

WRITER
He, Him, His   **He or She, Him or Her, His or Her**

APPENDIX II
Misused Phrases and Salutations

Examples of misused phrases and salutations:

Wrong	*Right*
Corporate Wives	**Corporate Spouses**
Faculty Wives	**Faculty Spouses**
Farmer and His Wife	**Farm Couple;** **Farmer and His or Her Spouse**
Man and Wife	**Husband and Wife;** **Man and Woman**
Senate Wives	**Senate Spouses**
Service Wives	**Service Spouses**
Working Wives	**Working Spouses**

Wrong	Right
Dear Madam	**Omit Salutation; Resident; Greetings**
Dear Miss	**Omit Salutation; Dear Ms.**
Dear Mrs.	**Omit Salutation; Dear Ms.**
Dear Sir	**Omit Salutation; Resident; Greetings**
Gentlemen	**Omit Salutation; Resident; Greetings**

APPENDIX III
Reference to Things, Places and Ideas

When referring to things, places and ideas, do not refer to them as male or female. If reference is necessary, repeat the word or use the right reference word, as in:

Wrong	*Right*
AIRPLANE She, Her, Her	It, It, Its
ANGEL She, Her, Her	It, It, Its
DEVIL He, Him, His	It, It, Its
EASTER BUNNY He, Him, His	It, It, Its
GOD He, Him, His	It, It, Its

Wrong	*Right*
HURRICANE She, Her, Her	It, It, Its
JUSTICE She, Her, Her	It, It, Its
PARIS She, Her, Her	It, It, Its
ROBOT He, Him, His	It, It, Its
SHIP She, Her, Her	It, It, Its
STATUE She, Her, Her	It, It, Its
TOOTH FAIRY She, Her, Her	It, It, Its
WITCH She, Her, Her	It, It, Its

APPENDIX IV
Reference to Indefinite Words

When referring to indefinite words, do not refer to them as male or female. If reference is necessary, repeat the word or use the right reference word, as in:

Wrong	*Right*	*Acceptable*
ANYBODY His	**His or Her**	Their
ANYONE His	**His or Her**	Their
EACH His	**His or Her**	Their
EITHER His	**His or Her**	Their
EVERYBODY His	**His or Her**	Their

Wrong	Right	Acceptable
EVERYONE		
His	**His or Her**	Their
NEITHER		
His	**His or Her**	Their
NO ONE		
His	**His or Her**	Their
SOMEBODY		
His	**His or Her**	Their
SOMEONE		
His	**His or Her**	Their